921
HAL

C1

Blassingame, Wyatt.

William F. Halsey,
five star admiral

921
HAL

C1

Blassingame, Wyatt.

William F. Halsey,
five star admiral

DATE	BORROWER'S NAME		434
SEP 18	J. Steffens		
OCT 2			208
SEP 16 1981	Andy E.		
OCT 13	S. Hasan		208
	M.		3/3

WILLIAM F.
HALSEY
Five Star Admiral

WILLIAM F.
HALSEY

Five Star Admiral

BY WYATT BLASSINGAME

ILLUSTRATED BY PERS CROWELL

GARRARD PUBLISHING COMPANY
CHAMPAIGN, ILLINOIS

For Wyatt Lurton Blassingame
With hope that reading about
it is as close as he need ever
come to war.

Picture credits:

United Press International: p. 11, 15, 69, 76, 101, 107, 109
U.S. Bureau of Ships: p. 1, 29
U.S. Navy Department: p. 2, 52, 62 (bottom), 87, 92, 96, 97
Wide World Photos: p. 38, 62 (top), 64, 66, 72

Map by Henri A. Fluchere

Contents

1. "They're Shooting at My Own Boys!"

Standing on the bridge of the aircraft carrier *Enterprise*, Vice Admiral William F. Halsey watched the planes take off. He was a solidly built man with square shoulders and a big head that made him seem always to lean a little forward. Now his head turned slowly as he watched the planes lumber down the flight deck, gain speed, then lift cleanly into the air and head east toward Pearl Harbor, some 200 miles away.

The rising sun was just clear of the horizon; the sky was blue except for a few pink-tinted clouds. Halsey turned to Commander Miles Browning, his chief of staff. "It looks as if we are going to have a beautiful day."

"Yes, sir. By the time we reach Pearl this afternoon, I expect those pilots who just took off will all be swimming at the beach."

Halsey laughed. "Maybe I'll join them, when we get there. Right now I think I'll take a bath and get ready for breakfast."

He went to his quarters. There was a calendar on his desk, and he glanced at it as he undressed. The day was Sunday, December 7, 1941. For months there had been talk of a possible war with Japan, but this morning the United States was still at peace. Halsey was not thinking of trouble while he bathed and shaved, put on a freshly pressed uniform and newly shined shoes. He did not wear fancy uniforms as some high ranking officers did, but his plain khakis were always crisply pressed. His junior officers often joked about the amount of time it took him to dress each morning.

Though he had been up at dawn to see the planes off, it was almost eight before Halsey sat down for breakfast. Lieutenant Douglas Moulton, the flag secretary, was the only other officer in the ward room, and he jumped to his feet as the admiral entered.

"Sit down," Halsey said gruffly. "How many times have I got to tell you—don't stand up when I come to meals."

"Yes, sir," Moulton said, grinning. He knew Halsey

said the same thing every day — and every day his staff officers stood up when he entered.

Halsey was drinking his second cup of coffee when the phone rang. Lieutenant Moulton answered it. Halsey heard him say, "What? *What?*" Then Moulton dropped the phone. "Admiral," he gasped, "the staff duty officer says he has a message that there's an air raid on Pearl!"

Halsey leaped to his feet. He knew that the planes he'd launched at daylight should just now be reaching Pearl Harbor; some jittery antiaircraft gunner must have mistaken them for Japanese. "They're shooting at my own boys!" he shouted. "Get the word to Admiral Kimmel in Pearl! Stop them!"

"Aye-aye, sir!" Moulton grabbed the phone. But at the same moment the door banged open and Lieutenant Commander Leonard Dow, the communications officer, rushed in. Without a word he dropped a dispatch in front of Halsey. It read:

From: CINCPAC (Commander in Chief, Pacific)
To: All ships present
AIR RAID ON PEARL HARBOR. THIS IS NO DRILL.

Halsey stared at the message. He had known that

war was possible; in fact, he had personally felt sure it would soon begin. But like most American officials, he had believed it would start with a Japanese attack on the Philippines, not Pearl Harbor. However, there was no time now to wonder.

"Sound general quarters," he told Moulton. "Pass the word to the crew."

"Aye-aye, sir."

Instants later the ship rocked to the clash and clang of general quarters. Startled sailors raced for their battle stations, as a second dispatch was received. Soon a third dispatch was placed in front of Admiral Halsey:

> From: CINCPAC
> To: All ships present
> HOSTILITIES WITH JAPAN COMMENCE WITH
> AIR RAID ON PEARL

There could no longer be any doubt, Halsey realized. The war had begun. The thing he had spent his life preparing for was here.

Bill Halsey could not remember a time when he had not dreamed of and planned on being a naval officer. His ancestors had been seagoing men for more than 200 years. His father, for whom he was named, was an officer in the U.S. Navy. Bill, Junior had been

Eleven-year-old Bill Halsey played football at the Pingry School in Elizabeth.

born in Elizabeth, New Jersey, on October 30, 1882, and most of his youth was spent moving from one navy base to another. His earliest memories were of visiting his father on various warships and learning to salute both the flag and the quarter-deck. All his life the sight of a ship filled him with a mingled sense of awe and mystery.

By the time he could read, young Bill Halsey knew

he wanted to go to the Naval Academy as his father had done. At this time a boy could enter the academy at fifteen. The problem was that appointments were made by congressmen, and Bill's father, who had spent much of his life at sea, knew no congressmen. However, the President also could make appointments, and when he was still only fourteen years old, Bill Halsey wrote to President William McKinley.

> Dear Sir:
> ...I want to ask you, if you have not already promised your appointments to the Naval Academy, that you will give me one. My father is a naval officer, and is at present navigator on the U.S.S. *Montgomery*....I know people do not like to give important positions such as this is away without knowing the person they are giving them to. But then you know that a naval officer would not keep his position long if he were not the right kind of a man....I have been with my father on shore and on ship board a great deal, and have always wanted to enter the Navy.

The fourteen-year-old boy ended his letter with

a bit of flattery for the newly elected President:

It is almost needless to congratulate you
on your grand victory which every good
American sees is for the best. It has been
told you so many times by men it is
hardly worth while for us boys to say it.
                    Yours respectively,
                    W. F. Halsey, Jr.

Despite the flattery, President McKinley did not answer the boy's letter. Young Bill Halsey continued his studies in preparatory school. Two years passed, and still he did not have an appointment to the Academy.

"I'm not giving up," Bill told his father. "I know another way to be a naval officer."

"How?"

"The navy always needs doctors. If I go to the University of Virginia and study medicine, then I can get in the navy as a doctor."

So, in the fall of 1899, Bill Halsey entered the University of Virginia. He did not study much. He went out for football, joined a fraternity, and had a fine time. But in his letters home he still wrote wistfully about wanting to go to the Naval Academy.

Finally Bill's mother decided to take a hand in

the matter. Having received an introduction to the President, she went to Washington, and arranged an appointment with him. She explained that her son had always dreamed of going to the academy as his father had done, but that the family had never lived in one place long enough to know local politicians. The President was their only hope.

"I have been praying that you would give him an appointment," Mrs. Halsey said. "I have been praying very sincerely."

The President was deeply touched. "Madam," he said, "your prayers have been answered." Then he began to grin. "But it will be up to your son to pass the entrance examinations."

"He'll pass them," Mrs. Halsey said.

Bill Halsey did pass them after cramming furiously, and on July 7, 1900, he was sworn in as a naval cadet.

2. The Worst Fullback the Navy Ever Had

Freshmen at the Naval Academy were called plebes. At seventeen — almost eighteen — Bill Halsey was older than most. He had been raised in the navy, his father was now a professor at the academy, so young Bill knew his way around. It was natural for the other plebes to look up to him as a man of vast experience. He was elected to several class offices, went out for football, and was so busy he didn't have much time left to study.

At the academy a grade of 4.0 was the same as 100, or perfect. A grade of 2.5 was only slightly better than 60 and barely passing. When Bill got his first grade in mechanics, it was only 2.28. His father looked at the report a long time, then looked at Bill. "You realize this is failing?" he said.

"Yes, sir."

"You know what will happen if you keep on failing? You will be expelled, after all the years of trying to get here."

"Yes, sir."

"It seems to me," his father said, "you are spending more time practicing football than studying. I think you ought to quit football."

"No, sir! I love football. I—"

"And your grades?"

"I've got a plan," Bill said. "I promise I'll pass mechanics."

Bill's plan was simple. He knew several other plebes who were having trouble with the same class; he also knew some who were very good at it. He got the whole group together, and night after night those who understood the subject tutored the poor students. When the next examination came, Bill passed it easily. He said nothing until the grades were posted, then went to his father's office. "I got my grade in mechanics," he said, trying to sound very casual.

"What was it?"

"A 3.98."

The Captain stared at him. Then his eyes began to

twinkle. "That's not quite perfect," he said. "But I suppose it's good enough to let you keep playing football."

Although Halsey was almost six feet tall, he weighed only 150 pounds. But he played football in the same way that later he would fight a war. He gave to it every atom of his strength and natural ability, once tackling a man so hard that both Halsey and the ball carrier went completely off the field and over a small fence. Despite his size, he played varsity fullback his last two years at the academy. During his senior year he was president of the Athletic Association, and won a trophy for the first classman "who has done most during the year for the promotion of athletics at the Naval Academy."

Even so, the football teams Halsey played on were not very good ones. In his four years at the academy, the navy never once won the annual game with army. Halsey sometimes said later that he had played on the worst teams in navy history.

Years later when Admiral William Halsey first met General of the Army Dwight D. Eisenhower the General's first words were, "Admiral, they tell me you claim to be the worst fullback who ever went to the Naval Academy."

It took Halsey by surprise. A little brusquely he said, "That's true. What about it?"

Eisenhower flashed his world-famous grin and stuck out his hand. "I want you to meet the worst halfback that ever went to the Military Academy," he said.

From that point on, the two men were friends.

Even more than football, young Bill Halsey enjoyed the summer cruises which all midshipmen at the academy had to make. He had been raised around ships, and he had a natural, almost instinctive skill at handling them. On his first summer cruise he displayed another natural ability that would help make his life at sea a happy one.

This first cruise was on an ancient, square-rigged sailing ship, the *Chesapeake*. When they had been at sea only a few days, the *Chesapeake* ran into a storm, and within an hour many of the regular crew were seasick, along with practically all the midshipmen. Not Halsey. Whipped by wind and rain, he climbed the mast to work at the sails, clinging to the rigging while the ship rolled, the mast swinging wildly until it almost touched the water, first on one side, then the other. With the sails furled and lashed into place, he climbed down without even becoming dizzy.

Many excellent officers have had to quit the navy because of seasickness. But in all his life, even on rolling destroyers and in typhoons, Bill Halsey was never seasick.

3. Round the World with the Great White Fleet

Bill Halsey was in his second year at the Naval Academy when Theodore Roosevelt became President. Roosevelt believed in a strong navy, and under his direction the government quickly began to build new ships. To man these, the course at the academy was speeded up, and Bill Halsey graduated in February rather than June, 1904. Immediately he was assigned to the battleship *Missouri*.

Halsey was barely on board when the *Missouri* sailed for winter training at Guantanamo, an American base in Cuba. With the arrival of spring, the fleet moved to Pensacola, Florida for target practice.

On Friday morning April 13, the *Missouri* was in the blue-green waters of the Gulf of Mexico. Off to

the west, barely visible on the horizon, another ship towed a barge with a high screen on it. This was the target for the *Missouri's* main battery of four 12-inch guns.

Halsey's battle station was on the bridge. When the *Missouri's* big guns fired, he could feel the ship shudder under his feet; flame and smoke flashed from the cannons' mouths, and the sound struck him like a physical blow. Watching through his glasses, he would try to spot the geysers where the shells struck near the target.

Suddenly, from one of the gun turrets, flame spurted skyward. It rose in a blinding flash, 400 feet against the blue sky, as the battleship reeled from an explosion greater than the firing of any guns. An instant later a second explosion followed.

In one of the turrets four ninety-pound bags of powder had blown up. Sparks flashed into the handling room below and set off twelve other bags. Five officers and twenty-six enlisted men were killed.

It was the first time Bill Halsey had ever seen death at sea. Sailors often tend to be superstitious, and Halsey could not get over the fact this accident happened on the 13th. From that day on he was extremely cautious about anything done on the 13th, especially if it was a Friday.

After a year on the *Missouri*, Halsey was ordered to the *Don Juan de Austria*. She sailed for the Caribbean, then returned to Norfolk for repairs. Here one day, Halsey was drilling a squad on deck when he noticed that the wife of the *Don Juan*'s executive officer had come on board and was standing nearby. With her was a very pretty girl with blue eyes and blonde hair. When the young ensign saw her watching him, he began to show off. His orders came louder and faster.

Suddenly something struck his head and knocked off his cap. He looked down and saw he had been hit by the girl's muff. He looked at the girl, and she was laughing so hard she had to hold on to the rail.

Halsey dismissed the men he had been drilling, then picked up the girl's muff. She reached for it, but Halsey backed away. "The only way you can get this," he said, "is to tell me your name and where you live."

Her name was Frances Grandy and she lived in Norfolk. Bill Halsey lost no time in calling at her home. After that he spent as much of his off duty time as possible with her.

He did not have long. Orders came sending him to the *Kansas*, a new battleship about to sail on a world cruise that would last for two years.

President Theodore Roosevelt wanted to show off the growing power of the U.S. Navy. He ordered sixteen battleships and five destroyers painted white as a symbol of peace. Then the Great White Fleet, as the papers called it, put to sea on a round-the-world tour. They visited Trinidad, Brazil, went around the Horn to Chile, westward across the Pacific to Australia, and then north to Japan.

In Japan the American officers were entertained on board ships of the Imperial Navy, and young Halsey got a glimpse of Admiral Count Heihachiro Togo, the commander of the Japanese fleet. Admiral Togo was famous for having started a war with Russia by attacking Russian ships while they lay at anchor before war was declared. Togo had also started a war with China by sinking a troopship without notice. To Bill Halsey this type of treacherous action seemed typical of the whole Japanese nation. It created in him a bitterness and hatred that he never forgot.

From Japan, the Great White Fleet sailed southwest through the China Sea, then west and north across the Indian Ocean, the Red Sea, the Mediterranean, and home across the Atlantic.

This cruise marked a change in Bill Halsey's life. He was growing up. He enjoyed his shore leave in all the cities he visited, and he wrote letters to Frances Grandy from every port but he was also learning to make use of the long hours at sea. He spent many of them reading and studying and when he was back in the United States he took an examination for promotion.

The exam lasted for six days, eight hours a day. Bill Halsey was one of seven officers who took the test; he was one of four who passed. Normally he would have been promoted to lieutenant junior grade; but because there was an opening available, he was jumped two ranks to full lieutenant.

Proud of the new wide stripe on his sleeve and his new pay, Halsey proposed to Frances Grandy. On December 1, 1909 they were married in Christ Church, in Norfolk. Bill Halsey wore his full dress uniform, and Frances cut the wedding cake with a sword.

4. World War I

During the early years of his marriage the navy assigned Halsey to various jobs, some on shore and some at sea. During one tour of sea duty he was ordered to take the destroyer *Flusser* to Campobello Island, off the coast of Maine. Here he was to report to the Assistant Secretary of the Navy, a tall, handsome young man named Franklin Delano Roosevelt.

Roosevelt and Halsey were almost exactly the same age and they hit it off from the first. But when Roosevelt said, "I know these waters well, so I'll pilot you through the strait between here and the mainland," Halsey hesitated. A destroyer is no ship for an amateur sailor to handle. Still, Roosevelt was Assistant Secretary of the Navy.

"Very well," Halsey said slowly. But when he turned the steering control over to Roosevelt, Halsey stood close behind him.

For a few minutes the going was easy. Then, as the destroyer rounded a point of land into narrow waters, Halsey saw Roosevelt turn swiftly to watch the way the stern of the ship swung, then stop the swing at just the right moment. With a sigh of relief Halsey said, "Mr. Secretary, I was afraid you might think this destroyer handled like some pleasure boat. But I see you know your business."

Roosevelt began to laugh. "I knew you were afraid I'd put us aground. That's why you were standing so close to me, and I don't blame you."

It was the beginning of a friendship that lasted until Roosevelt's death while President of the United States.

Not long after Halsey's first meeting with Roosevelt, World War I began in Europe. The United States was still at peace, but German submarines were operating close to the American coast. Bill Halsey, now skipper of the destroyer *Jarvis*, was assigned to patrol duty off New York harbor.

On one patrol, the *Jarvis* met heavy fog through which it had to run a zigzag course up and down the coast. The fog lasted all day, all night, and into the next day. Not once could the navigator see the sun or stars to get an accurate fix on the ship's position. With only a vague idea of his location, Halsey stayed on the bridge for hour after hour.

Suddenly—he did not know why—he had an overwhelming sense of danger. He could see nothing except the fog. The only sounds were the steady throb of the engines and the dull mutter of waves against the ship's hull. Everything seemed exactly as it had for more than 24 hours. Yet he had a sudden and terrible sense of danger.

"Full speed astern!" Halsey shouted.

The destroyer shuddered and lost way. Nearby Halsey made out the blur of a small fishing boat. He shouted, "Can you give me my position?"

Back came the voice of the fisherman. "If you keep going for half a mile, you'll be right in the middle of the Fire Island Life Saving Station!"

"Thank you," Halsey said. "But I think I'll turn around."

He would never know what had warned him of danger. Perhaps it was only the instinct of a born sailor, a kind of "feeling" that told him the water was shallow.

From the *Jarvis* Halsey was assigned to duty at the Naval Academy. He was here in 1917 when the United States entered World War I. Immediately he asked for sea duty and early the next year was given command of the destroyer *Benham*.

The *Benham*'s job was to accompany groups of merchant ships and to protect them from German submarines. Halsey escorted ships westward from French and English ports until they were 500 miles or so across the Atlantic and beyond the area where German submarines operated most frequently. Then the *Benham* would swing around, join an eastbound convoy, and protect it back into port.

Weather was often an even greater danger than enemy submarines. Winter storms lashed the North Atlantic. Gigantic waves of icy water would pour over the little destroyer's bow, crash against her bridge and sweep along her deck, carrying overboard any unsecured gear or careless sailors. On stormy nights many ships were unable to hold their position in the convoy. In the pitch darkness, sailing without lights, there was always the danger of collision. Many nights Halsey was on the bridge from darkness until dawn, without rest.

Even during calm weather there was the constant strain of searching for submarines. One dark night Halsey was leaning over the rail when he saw a stream of phosphorescent bubbles streaking toward the *Benham*'s bow. Instinctively he shouted, "Torpedo!" though already it was too close to swing the ship away. He could only hold his breath and wait for the explosion.

Close against the destroyer's bow the bubbles went suddenly deeper—and vanished. There was no

Halsey was skipper of the U.S.S. *Benham*, above, on
escort duty in the perilous North Atlantic.

explosion. Halsey rushed to the other side of the
bridge, saw the glowing bubbles rise and flash into
the air like tiny fireworks.

With a gasp of relief he realized it was a porpoise,
not a torpedo. Even in daylight it was often difficult
to tell one from the other.

Before dawn one June morning, Halsey was asleep
in his cabin when a radioman shook him awake.
"Captain, we just got a message from a British patrol
ship. She's bombed a German sub that sank a ship
eight miles off Trevose Head."

This was not far from Halsey's present position and
he gave orders for the destroyer to turn up flank
speed, heading east. As the sun rose ahead of him, he

saw two P-boats and two trawlers searching for the sub. Overhead two British planes and a blimp were also searching.

As his own ship prowled back and forth, Halsey watched the planes. He had never thought much about the use of airplanes in naval warfare, but watching these, it was obvious they could cover far more territory than his destroyer. The idea stayed fixed in the back of his mind.

More than two hours passed and there was no sign of the sub. Halsey swung west again to rejoin his own convoy. At midmorning he was in the charthouse when he heard a lookout shout, "Submarine on the surface dead ahead!"

Halsey leaped for the bridge. There, low in the water, was a submarine. The destroyer's forward gun was already manned, the gunner's finger on the trigger. Halsey was about to give the order to fire when the quartermaster, who was peering through glasses, shouted, "Captain, that's an American sub!"

Halsey grabbed the glasses. Even then he could see only a fish-like outline with the conning tower dark above it. "Fire the recognition signal," he ordered.

Flares rose above the destroyer, but there was no answer from the sub. It lay still in the water, the destroyer bearing swiftly down upon it. Once more

Halsey was about to give the order to fire, but his quartermaster said, "She's American, sir. I can see the markings on her."

Moments later the sub fired her recognition signal. And finally Halsey, too, could see the letters on the conning tower. The sub was American all right.

Shaking his head, Halsey turned to the quartermaster. In his excitement he had not really noticed who the man was. Now he recognized him. He was a full-blooded American Indian.

Halsey began to laugh. "I've always heard about Indians' eyesight. Now I'll believe it."

This action may have been as close as Bill Halsey got to attacking an "enemy" submarine in World War I. He dropped depth charges on unknown objects that may or may not have been submarines. But throughout the course of the entire war, he was never sure he actually saw or hit one.

5. Test Failed

In peacetime the life of a naval officer usually alternates between duty at sea and duty on shore. In the years after World War I, Bill Halsey had a number of assignments, including service on a number of destroyers, on the battleship *Wyoming*, and at times in Washington at what he called an LSD— a "large steel desk" in an office. His family was growing: he had a daughter, Margaret, and a son, William F. Halsey III. Young Bill, like his father and grandfather, wanted to go to the Naval Academy. But because of his eyes, young Bill would never be able to pass the physical examination.

Navy promotions in peacetime are always slow, but in 1927 when he was forty-five years old, Halsey was made captain. He was assigned to duty at the

Naval Academy as commanding officer of the *Reina Mercedes*, anchored nearby. He and his family lived aboard the ship. Also on board the *Reina* was the navy's first permanent aviation detail with Lieutenant DeWitt "Duke" Ramsey, as its senior officer.

A few days after taking command of the *Reina*, Halsey called on Lieutenant Ramsey. "Duke," he said, "as C.O. I'm responsible for everything here, and I don't like to be responsible for something I don't understand. I wish you would educate me on this aviation business."

"Fine, Captain. Let's go flying."

The plane looked like some strange, two-winged kite, but it flew. And Captain Halsey, leaning over the side, peering down at the Academy buildings, at the long blue stretch of Chesapeake Bay dotted with ships, was totally fascinated. Over the roar of the engine he began to shout questions at Duke Ramsey.

Back on the *Reina* Halsey kept on with his questions. He persuaded Ramsey to take him flying, time and again. He learned to take the controls himself once the plane was safely in the air, and he began to dream of the role aviation could play in naval warfare. Before long he began to drop hints to senior officers that he himself would like to have an assignment in aviation.

The chance came in 1930. He could take the course at the Naval Air School at Pensacola—if he could pass the physical examination.

Bill Halsey was forty-eight years old now, with grown children, but he was in good physical condition. Since entering the navy, he had taken physical examinations regularly and passed them all without trouble. He had no doubt he could pass this one. But when the doctor examining his eyes said, "Read the third line from the bottom of the chart," Halsey found the letters looked blurred. He leaned forward. He squinted. But the letters refused to come clear, and Captain Halsey failed the eye test for naval aviation. Instead of being sent to the air school, he was given command of a squadron of destroyers in the Atlantic.

At this point Halsey felt sure he would never have a career in aviation. But it still fascinated him. He remembered the planes he had seen hunting for German submarines, and he studied new ways to use planes assigned to the fleet. When his destroyers practiced torpedo attacks, Halsey sent planes to track the torpedoes. Half the time he would watch from the bridge of his flagship, but the other half the time he flew with the pilot doing the tracking.

After this tour of duty Halsey was sent to the Naval War College and a year later to the Army War College.

In both places he worked on plans to improve the use of aircraft in combat.

Then without warning came the break. It was a letter from Admiral Ernest J. King, Chief of the Bureau of Aeronautics, and it offered Halsey command of the aircraft carrier *Saratoga*. Only again there was an if—if he could pass the aviation observers course at Pensacola, Florida. As an observer rather than a pilot, he would not be required to pass the eye examination, but it was still a long, rough course for a man fifty-one years old. Did he want to try?

Joyfully Halsey wrote to Admiral King accepting the offer. He kissed his wife good-bye, got in his car, and headed for Pensacola. This was a three-day trip, and the last night along the way he spent in Tallahassee. He was undressing in his hotel when suddenly he began to say to himself, "Bill, you're fifty-one years old and a grandfather. Tomorrow morning you'll be competing with youngsters less than half your age!"

He made up his mind. For as long as he was in flight school he would quit drinking and smoking. He would go in training like a prizefighter getting ready for a championship match. He might be middle-aged, but he would put himself in top physical condition, and he would pass the course no matter how tough it was.

6. Flight School

Squadron 1, the beginners' squadron at the Pensacola Flight School, gathered in the hangar for its first lecture. Except for Captain Halsey, all the students were ensigns or lieutenants junior grade, boys in their late teens or early twenties. They glanced uneasily at the gray-haired, rugged-faced man sitting in the front row. What was a captain, a man with 30 years' experience in the navy, doing here as a student?

Bill Halsey was aware of their glances and whispers. He didn't blame them. My own son's as old as any one of them, he thought.

The instructor was a lieutenant, not much older than the students. He was obviously uneasy as he outlined the course. In Squadron 1, he said, students would spend half the day at ground school, half the day flying. In ground school they would study engines, navigation, and radio. The flying would be basic, primary training. An aviation observer, he carefully pointed out, would not be required to learn actual flying, only the theory.

When the class broke up for its first flight, the instructor approached Halsey. "Captain, Lieutenant Bromfield Nichol will be your personal instructor. I'll have an enlisted man here each day to carry your parachute to the plane. And—"

"Now wait," Halsey said, looking around him. "The other students are carrying their own chutes."

"Yes, sir, but—"

"No," Halsey said. "Let's get one thing clear. I don't want any special favors. I'm a student here and I want to be treated as one."

"Yes, sir, but—"

"No buts, and no favors. I mean it."

He did, and he stuck to it—though there was one exception a few days later. After he had been flying a few days with Lieutenant Nichol, he asked to take over the controls. His eyes were no longer as keen as they had been, but his reflexes were still good. He found he could handle the plane, and after this he went to the commanding officer of the school. "If

The *Saratoga* in 1934. Halsey was slated to be skipper
of the navy's great aircraft carrier.

I'm going to be skipper of a carrier," Halsey said,
"I want to know all I can about the way pilots think
and the problems they face. I can learn more by
actually flying than by being an observer. I want my
designation changed from student observer to
student pilot, and I want to take the pilot's course."

"What about the eye test, Captain?"

"Well...."

Years later five-star Admiral Halsey would write
that he never did know how it was done or by whom.

But somewhere up the chain of command someone managed to forget that Halsey had failed his eye examination. And Captain William Halsey, fifty-one years old, became a "student pilot."

At first Halsey tried to conceal the fact that he needed glasses, and on at least one occasion this got him in trouble. This was a group navigational flight where the student pilots took turns leading the way, and Halsey was to lead the last leg of the flight back to the airfield. The compass was mounted in the front cockpit; Halsey, as student, sat in the rear, and from there, without his glasses, he could not read the compass. With all the other planes following, he headed in the wrong direction. His instructor let him go until the gas began to drop low in the gauge. Then he turned and shouted, "Captain, the field is back that way!"

After this Halsey had his prescription glasses built into his goggles.

The beginning squadron trained in seaplanes, and regulations required that a pilot solo after not less than eight or more than twelve hours of instruction. Student Halsey took the full twelve. But finally came the day when he climbed into his seaplane alone and taxied slowly away from the ramp. In the bay crash boats were ready and waiting. From the ramp the commanding officer of the flight school watched nervously. He believed the captain could fly all right, but still—

The plane picked up speed. The pontoons flung spray high in the air. The plane lifted, wobbled slightly, then sailed away down the bay. Fifteen minutes later it was back again, touching down for a fairly smooth landing. Halsey taxied back to the ramp and climbed out, grinning like a twelve-year-old boy.

Waiting for him were all the members of his flight class. It was a custom that the last man to solo in each class got thrown into the bay, and Captain Halsey had been the last. Still, treating a fifty-one-year-old captain like an ensign was something else. The youngsters hesitated.

"Hello, gentlemen," Halsey said.

"Good afternoon, sir," they replied faintly.

He grinned at them. "Well, what are you waiting for?"

With a roar they rushed at him, grabbed him by the arms and legs, swung, and let go. Telling about it later and laughing until he could hardly speak, Halsey said, "Those kids threw me so far, I thought I was going to need a life raft to get back."

From Squadron 1, Halsey and his class moved to Squadron 2 and primary land-training planes. With Squadron 3 they began to use actual service planes.

These were still comparatively slow biplanes, but because they had a free-swiveling tail wheel, they were inclined to loop easily. One day while Halsey was in the air, a summer squall blew up. Wind and rain lashed the field, but with his gas running low, Halsey signaled that he was coming in for a landing.

On the field sirens screamed. Ambulances and fire equipment rushed out. Men held their breath as Halsey's plane swooped over the trees at the end of the airstrip, swerved in the fierce wind, righted itself—and came in for a perfect landing.

A few days later in lovely weather, Halsey brought his plane in, but it seemed to hang in the air until he was three-quarters of the distance down the runway. It hit and ground-looped. Neither he nor the plane were hurt, but Lieutenant Nichol, who was watching, said, "I don't understand it. The worse the weather, the better the captain flies. And the better the weather, the worse he flies."

Whenever a student pulled an obvious boner like taxiing his plane into a boundary light, he was given the Flying Jackass Award. This was an aluminum figure of a donkey, and the student pilot had to wear it on his chest until another student did something to "win" it away from him. When Captain Halsey ran his plane into a boundary light, he was given the Flying Jackass and wore it for ten days before another student won it. Told it was time to give it up, Halsey hesitated. "Could we have another one made?" he asked. "I won't wear this one anymore; but I would like to keep it. When I get to be skipper of the *Saratoga*, I'll hang it in my cabin. Then when some pilot pulls a stupid stunt, I'll look at it before I bawl him out. It'll remind me that I've done some pretty stupid things too."

Although he would never become a truly good pilot, Bill Halsey did become a fair one, and in May 1935 he graduated along with the rest of his class. There would be few prouder moments in his life than when the wings of a naval aviator were pinned on his chest.

7. War Begins

When Bill Halsey took command of the *Saratoga*, it was based at Long Beach, California. From its flight deck he could see Japanese tankers taking on cargoes of American oil, day after day. He could see Japanese merchant ships loading scrap iron for shipment to Japan.

The sight infuriated Captain Halsey. "Someday," he told his junior officers, "we are going to get that scrap iron back in the shape of bombs and shells."

Like many naval officers, Halsey was convinced, even in 1935, that a future war with Japan was more than likely. But it was not this alone which angered him when he saw American cargoes leaving for Japan. Bill Halsey hated the Japanese with a deep, personal hatred that he himself did not understand. Perhaps it stemmed from his memory of Admiral

Togo's peacetime attacks on Russian and Chinese ships. "The Japanese," Halsey told anyone who would listen, "are a tricky, treacherous people. Some day they are likely to attack us without warning, just as they did the Russians."

But in 1935 and 1936 the United States remained at peace. In 1937 Halsey was transferred back to Pensacola, this time as commandant of the Naval Air Station. He served there a year, was promoted to Rear Admiral, and placed in command of the carriers *Yorktown* and *Enterprise*, plus the cruisers and destroyers that operated with them. Then, as American relations with Japan grew steadily worse, Halsey and his carriers were ordered from the Atlantic to the Pacific, based at Pearl Harbor.

Several years before this, Japan had invaded China, who was at that time friendly to the United States. The U.S. protested, but without success. Then in September 1939, World War II started in Europe. Germany and Japan, although not actual allies at the time, were friendly, while American sympathies lay with England and France. Japanese warlords talked openly of conquering the Philippines which belonged to the U.S. As relations grew steadily worse, officials in Washington sent a secret message to the commanding officers of the army and navy in Hawaii that Japan might start a war at any time.

This message reached Hawaii on November 27, 1941. That same morning Halsey, now a Vice Admiral, was summoned to the Pearl Harbor office of Admiral Husband Kimmel, the commanding naval officer in the Pacific. Several other admirals were present, along with army and marine corps generals.

On the wall of Kimmel's office was a huge map of the Pacific. On it the Admiral pointed to two small islands owned by the U.S., west of Hawaii. "As you know," Kimmel said, "we have only recently begun to fortify Wake and Midway. Airfields are complete, but as yet the islands have no planes. What I wanted to discuss with you gentlemen is the type of planes we should send."

General Walter Short, the army's commanding general of the Hawaiian Department, answered quickly. "If the Japanese attack Hawaii, these planes will be the first to meet them. So we should send the best we have."

General Short was referring to his own fighters, but Halsey asked, "Is it true, General, that your fighters are ordered not to go more than fifteen miles from shore?"

"That's correct," Short said. "Our pilots are not trained to navigate over water."

"Then we will need navy or marine pilots," Halsey said.

Both Short and Admiral Kimmel agreed, and the decision was made to send F4F planes with marine pilots. Using the *Enterprise*, Halsey would take the planes and pilots going to Wake, while another admiral would carry those going to Midway. "Do it as secretly as possible," Kimmel ordered. "We don't want the Japs to know we are arming these islands."

Early the next morning the *Enterprise* steamed out of Pearl Harbor and turned east, toward the United States. This was to confuse any Japanese spies who might be watching. Even the marine pilots destined for Wake had been told they were merely going to sea for a few days drill. But once over the horizon, the *Enterprise* swung westward toward Wake, and the waves at her bow curled high as she picked up speed.

With Hawaii well behind, Halsey issued Battle Order Number 1. It began:

1. The *Enterprise* is now operating under war conditions.
2. At any time, day or night, we must be ready for instant action.
3. Hostile submarines may be encountered. . . .

Then came the real jolt. Pilots flying search patterns

ALEUTIAN ISLANDS

Pacific

Ocean

UNITED

STATES

San Francisco •

Midway

HAWAIIAN ISLANDS

Oahu

Pearl Harbor

(1)

1. Japanese Attack on Pearl Harbor
   Dec. 7, 1941

2. Air Attack on the Gilbert and Marshall Islands — Jan. 31–Feb. 1, 1942

3. Colonel Doolittle's Attack on Tokyo
   April 18, 1942

4. Battle of Guadalcanal — Fall, 1942

5. Battle of Leyte Gulf — Oct. 23–26, 1944

6. Kamikaze Attacks on Task Force 38
   November, 1944

7. Disablement of Task Force 38 by a
   Typhoon — Dec. 17–18, 1944

8. Air Attacks on Japan from Task Force
   38 — July 28–Aug. 14, 1945

FIJI
ISLANDS

SAMOA

Ocean

Pacific

ahead of the *Enterprise*, Halsey ordered, would sink any ships they saw and shoot down any planes.

Commander William Buracker, Halsey's Operations Officer, stared at the order in amazement, then rushed to the Admiral's quarters. "Admiral," he cried, "did you authorize this?"

"Yes," Halsey said.

"You realize that this means war?"

"Yes."

Buracker still could not believe what he was hearing. "But you can't start a private war, Admiral. Who's going to take the responsibility?"

"I will," Halsey said. He struck the top of his desk with his fist. "I have already made certain that no American or Allied shipping is in this area. Anything we find will be Japanese, and we don't want the Japs to know we are taking these planes to Wake. So if we find any Japanese ships, I want them sunk before they can get off a radio message."

Fortunately, or unfortunately, no Japanese ships were encountered. The great Japanese fleet that would strike the surprise blow at Pearl Harbor was already at sea, well to the north of Halsey's location, although he had no way of knowing this. If the *Enterprise* had found and attacked Japanese ships on the open sea, the United States might have been blamed for starting the war. On the other hand, such an attack might have alerted the Hawaiian defenses, readying them for the planes that caught them unprepared on December 7.

No one can say. The *Enterprise* steamed westward over empty seas, delivered the marine planes to Wake, and turned east again. Her schedule called for her to enter Pearl Harbor at seven o'clock Sunday morning, December 7, but rough seas slowed her. At daylight that morning, she was still some 200 miles away. Halsey ordered eighteen planes to take off and search ahead of the ship, just as they did every morning at sea. But instead of returning to the *Enterprise*, they would continue on to Pearl Harbor.

From the flag bridge Halsey watched his planes depart, then went to his quarters to bathe, shave, and change his uniform. Later he was sitting down at breakfast when the dispatch came:

AIR RAID ON PEARL HARBOR. THIS IS NO DRILL.

After that dispatches came in a flood. All ships at sea were ordered to rendezvous with Halsey's task force, under his command. They would search for and strike the Japanese fleet. But nobody knew where that fleet was. Some reports had it to the north, some to the south, some to the west. Halsey's small force raced first in one direction, then another. He

At Pearl Harbor, December 7, 1941—billowing smoke
and destruction on Battleship Row. At the right is the
Oklahoma, capsized and sinking.

knew that if he did find the enemy he would be vastly outnumbered, but he paced the bridge as if he could find the Japanese simply by stalking up and down.

Over the horizon came an ancient four-stacked destroyer racing straight westward. As it tore past, Halsey signaled, "Where are you headed?"

Back came the answer. "Don't know. My orders are to steam west at top speed."

"Join up," Halsey ordered, and turned to Commander Miles Browning. "It's a good thing we saw him. The way he was going, if his fuel held out, he'd wind up on the China coast."

It was a typical remark. Even in moments of great stress, Bill Halsey could still joke.

No one found the Japanese fleet, now safely on its way back to Japan. And the next day, his fuel dangerously low, Halsey returned to Pearl Harbor. It was late dusk when the *Enterprise* moved up the channel, but Halsey could see the glow of still burning fires and the wreckage of sunken ships. One of these was the battleship *Utah*, sunk at her berth. It was the same berth the *Enterprise* would have occupied had she reached Pearl Harbor on schedule the day before.

8. First Carrier Strikes

As days passed with no new attack, it became obvious that, for a time at least, the Hawaiian Islands were safe. Admiral Chester Nimitz, newly appointed Commander in Chief of the Navy in the Pacific, sent for Halsey. "Bill," Nimitz said, "it looks as if the Japs may plan to drive across the Central Pacific toward Samoa. If they do, that will cut our line of communications with Australia and New Zealand."

Nimitz went on to explain that reinforcements were being sent to the island of Samoa from the United States. Still other troops would be sent from Hawaii. "Your task force is to escort those from here," Nimitz said. "After you put the marines ashore in Samoa, you'll turn northwest and hit the Japanese in the Gilbert and Marshall Islands. If we can hurt them there, it will make any Japanese attack on Samoa far more difficult."

Smiling grimly Halsey studied the charts spread on Nimitz' desk. His job was not going to be an easy one. For many years the Japanese had not allowed ships from other nations to visit the Gilbert and Marshall Islands. Consequently little was known about them. Even the surrounding waters were poorly charted. But it was a job that needed to be done. On the night of January 31, their Samoan mission completed, Halsey's ships began the final approach to the Japanese islands. There was a full moon; the sea was calm; behind each racing ship the wake stretched like a silver ribbon. Standing on the flag bridge of the *Enterprise,* Halsey could feel his nerves growing tighter and tighter. But he knew that as the commanding officer he should appear calm, and his face showed nothing. Indeed, he looked so cool that when he said he was going to his cabin and sleep, his officers believed him.

Actually he could not sleep but only rolled and tossed.

The admiral commanding a task force has nothing to do with the operation of the individual ship on which he sails. This is left to the ship's captain. But the admiral does direct the entire task force, and the place where most of his work is done is called flag plot. On the *Enterprise,* flag plot was a large room high above the flight deck and jammed with equipment. Loudspeakers brought messages from all parts of the ship. Instruments showed the ship's speed, direction, and location. The location of other ships in the force and of planes in the air were also shown. Messengers came and went in a constant stream. Yeomen typed out every word of radio talk and orders given.

Circling flag plot on three sides was the flag bridge, an open, horseshoe-shaped platform that gave a view in every direction. About midnight when Halsey gave up trying to sleep, he went first to flag plot, then the bridge, wandering restlessly back and forth.

All night the ships raced closer to the Japanese islands. By 0400 (4:00 A.M.) the nearest island lay just beyond the horizon. Halsey knew that in bringing his ships this close to the enemy, he was taking a chance many commanders would have considered foolhardy. It not only made it easy for Japanese planes to find his ships, but there was also the danger of hitting a mine or even going aground. But it also made it possible for him to strike hard, and, from first to last, Bill Halsey believed in striking with all his power.

With the first gray light of dawn, the *Enterprise* swung into the wind and began to launch her planes.

Minutes later the first American bombs began to fall on Japanese territory.

All morning Halsey kept his ships swinging back and forth so close to one island that the towering smoke of fires and bursting bombs could be seen from the bridge. All morning planes dropped their bombs, came back for more, and took off again. Every man knew that sooner or later Japanese bombers would find the American ships. In fact, no one could understand why the ships had not been attacked already.

In the early afternoon one pilot reported to Halsey on his last mission, then said, "Admiral, don't you think it's time we hauled out of here?"

"My boy," Halsey said, "I was just thinking the same thing." The ships swung eastward, and the bow waves grew high as they turned up flank speed.

At this point the Japanese planes found them. Off the starboard bow appeared five twin-engine bombers, all heading for the *Enterprise*. At the same moment the antiaircraft guns of the entire force went into action. Tracers rose in long, gently curving arcs; bursting five-inch shells made a black wall across the sky. But the bombers came through it, changing course to follow the twisting course of the *Enterprise*.

From the flag bridge Halsey saw the planes' bomb bays open, saw the bombs slide out, seem to hang motionless for a moment, and arch downward at the

ship. "Hit the deck!" someone yelled. Then Halsey, along with everyone else, flung himself flat. Joking about it later, he would say that he was the "fustest and the flattest."

The bombs missed, though one was so close alongside, it cut a gasoline line, starting a small fire. As helmeted sailors rushed to put out the fire, Halsey glanced upward and saw that one of the bombers had swung around and was heading back. Both its engines were on fire, but somehow it managed to stay in the air.

Once more the AA guns went into action. The red tracers arched upward, vanishing into the body of the plane. But still it came on, the pilot obviously meaning to crash his burning plane into the ship. To Halsey and to all the men on the flag bridge it seemed as if the pilot aimed straight at them. Once more the men hurled themselves flat.

At the last moment, the *Enterprise*'s captain swung his ship hard to starboard. The burning plane tried to follow, but most of its controls were gone now. The plane hit the flight deck a glancing blow, bounced, and went over the side into the sea.

Admiral Halsey got to his feet, breathing hard. He noticed that one of the enlisted men standing nearby was grinning. Halsey turned to Commander Miles Browning. "Miles," he demanded, "who is that man?"

Browning was slow to answer. "Sir," he said, "that's yeoman first class Ira Bowman."

"No," Halsey said, "he's chief yeoman now. Any man who can grin like that when my knees are shaking is due a promotion."

A few days later Halsey's task force re-entered Pearl Harbor, met by wildly cheering sailors. Actually, from the military point of view, the blow against the Gilbert and Marshall Islands had not amounted to much. But it had come at a time when all over the world Allied forces seemed to be losing the war. It proved that the United States could take the offensive, and it was a great boost to morale.

There were other raids against small Japanese islands. Then in March, Admiral Chester Nimitz once more sent for Halsey. What was being planned this time, Nimitz said, would be one of the most spectacular operations of the entire war, if it came off. "We are going to bomb Tokyo."

Halsey sat bolt upright in his chair. "Tell me about it."

The raid, Admiral Nimitz said, could not be done by navy planes, since these did not have sufficient range. But for several months the army had been training the crews of sixteen twin-engine bombers to take off from a carrier. The navy's job would be to get these men and planes within 400 miles or so of Japan. From that point they could fly over Tokyo, drop their bombs, and fly on to land in China, if everything went well. "Are you willing to take them out there?" Nimitz asked.

"I am," Halsey said.

The army bombers were loaded on the carrier *Hornet*, but Halsey, in command of the entire task force, stayed on the *Enterprise*. Everything depended on getting close enough to Japan to launch the planes before the ships were sighted. Without knowing it, he followed much the same course the Japanese fleet had taken to reach Pearl Harbor.

By the 17th of April the force was 1000 miles east of Tokyo. At this point the destroyers and tankers were left behind; the two carriers with a screen of cruisers began to race straight west. There was still no sign of enemy ships, but early the next morning a small Japanese picket ship was sighted. Before it could be sunk, it got off a radio message.

In flag plot, Halsey stared at the chart. He was still 650 miles from Tokyo. In his attack on the Gilberts he had brought his ships almost within sight of land, but an attack on the Japanese mainland was something else altogether. Here the enemy planes that might come looking for him would be numbered not by ones and twos, but by hundreds. Japanese carriers, battleships, and submarines would be

Doolittle's B-25's stacked on the flight deck of the
Hornet, enroute to the daring raid on Tokyo. Below,
a B-25 takes off—the next stop Japan!

swarming out to attack him. Regretfully, he sent a message to Admiral Mitscher commanding the *Hornet*: "Launch planes. To Colonel Doolittle and his gallant command good luck and God bless you."

From the bridge of the *Enterprise*, Halsey watched the army planes, with Colonel Doolittle's leading the way, take off and head for Japan. Then the American task force turned east. Every man on the ships was thinking about the flyers, wondering what would happen to them. Radios were tuned to Japan and the sailors stood in groups, listening.

In flag plot, Halsey heard a Japanese announcer, speaking in English, say that of all the warring countries in the world, Japan was the only one that could never be attacked—and just then, over the radio, came the sound of the air-raid siren.

Like the raid on the Marshall Islands, the attack on Tokyo did not amount to much from a military point of view. But in the United States it changed the entire spirit of the people. Now everyone knew this country could strike back, and, sooner or later, the tide of the war would change. This flight of Doolittle and his men, Halsey said, "was one of the most courageous deeds in all military history."

9. Guadalcanal and the South Pacific

The strain of long weeks at sea with almost no rest was beginning to tell on Admiral Halsey. He had lost weight, and by the time he returned from the raid on Tokyo his body had broken out in a rash that itched day and night. Admiral Nimitz said, jokingly, "Bill Halsey is just itching for a fight," but the *Enterprise*'s doctors sent Halsey ashore to the hospital at Pearl Harbor. From there he was sent back to a hospital in Virginia, and it was late fall before he could rejoin the fleet.

Meanwhile the great sea battle of Midway had been fought and won by the U.S. — the first truly big American victory of the war. With Midway, the Japanese chances for a drive across the Central Pacific were stopped, and not long afterward U.S. Marines invaded the Japanese-held island of Guadalcanal in the South Pacific. Here what actually started as a small-scale fight grew more and more fierce, and more and more important. If the U.S. could hold Guadalcanal, the Japanese drive toward Australia would be stopped. But if the U.S. lost the island, Australia and New Zealand were in grave danger.

On his return to the fleet, Halsey expected to be assigned to the command of a task force. First, however, he was sent on a flying tour of the South Pacific to familiarize himself with the area. At the island of Nouméa, headquarters of the South Pacific area and well behind the fighting, he was given a message marked "Secret." It was from CINCPAC and read:

YOU WILL TAKE COMMAND OF THE SOUTH PACIFIC AREA AND SOUTH PACIFIC FORCES IMMEDIATELY.

Halsey stared at it. This put him in command not only of all the ships in the area, but of the men fighting on Guadalcanal. The situation on Guadalcanal was desperate indeed, and Halsey knew nothing about working with ground forces. Still, it was the job that had been given to him. His eyes narrowed, his heavy jaw set, he went ashore and took over.

These marines searching for Japanese snipers on Guadalcanal were under Admiral Halsey's command.

His first act was to call a conference of the top officers already in the area. Quietly, Halsey listened to their stories. At this time the U.S. had only one aircraft carrier in the Solomon Islands area, opposed by a Japanese force of at least four carriers. Other U.S. ships were also outnumbered, though not so completely. Because of their carriers, and because they controlled other islands nearby, the Japanese controlled the sea and air around Guadalcanal. The U.S. Marines were not only short of men, they were short of ammunition, short of food, and almost without planes. Many of them were sick with malaria. They

were taking heavy casualties and needed reinforcements. But because of a lack of ships and planes,
it was difficult to get men and supplies to them.

When the story was complete, Halsey looked at
General Archie Vandegrift of the marines. "Archie,"
he said, "are we going to evacuate or hold?"

"I can hold," Vandegrift said, "but I've got to have
more active support than I've been getting."

"All right," Halsey said. "Go on back. I promise you
everything I've got."

Halsey knew the Japanese were preparing for an
all-out attack on Guadalcanal. The American plan
under Admiral Robert Ghormley, who had been
COMSOPAC before Halsey took over, had been to
conserve the few ships and planes in the area.
Halsey reversed this. He ordered the *Enterprise*, on
its way from Pearl Harbor with a small task force, to
make all possible speed. He moved his other fighting
ships forward to be ready for the Japanese attack.
When word came that the Japanese fleet was closing
in on Guadalcanal, Halsey sent an order to all his
forces that contained only three words:

ATTACK REPEAT ATTACK

What followed was not only one fight, but a whole
series of violent and bloody battles, ashore and at sea.

Within weeks, so many American, Australian, and Japanese ships were sunk that the waters around Guadalcanal became known as Ironbottom Sound.

As commanding officer of the entire area, Halsey could take no personal part in this fighting. But pacing his headquarters in Nouméa, knowing that close friends of many years were being killed, waiting for messages that were sometimes of victory and sometimes of defeat, was a far greater strain than standing on the flag bridge of the *Enterprise*.

It was during this time that Admiral Bill Halsey got a new name that would stay with him the rest of his life. Before this he had rarely if ever been interviewed by newspapers. But as the long, vicious fight for Guadalcanal wore on, newspapermen from all over the United States came to Halsey's headquarters. One of them asked, "Admiral, do you have a plan for ending the war?"

Halsey's bushy eyebrows pulled together and his eyes glittered. "I do," he said.

"How?"

"Kill Japs. Kill Japs. And keep on killing Japs."

Another reporter asked about the quality of the American fighting man compared to the Japanese. Halsey knew that after the Japanese victories early in the war, some reporters had referred to them as supermen. Now he glared at the reporter. "When the war started, I held one of our men equal to four Japs. I now increase this to twenty."

Hearing him bark his words and seeing his heavy jaw set like a bulldog's, the reporters began to refer to him not as Bill Halsey, but "Bull" Halsey. None of Halsey's personal friends ever called him this, but to the American public he became Bull Halsey, and the name stayed with him.

A month after Halsey took over as COMSOPAC he was promoted to full admiral. This brought him more to the attention of the American public than ever.

Admiral Halsey at work in his office at Nouméa, headquarters for the South Pacific command.

Meanwhile the vicious fighting over Guadalcanal continued, week after week. Gradually the terrible losses of ships, planes, and men became too heavy for the Japanese to bear. By February 9, 1943, the island was secure in American hands.

The fall of Guadalcanal marked one of the major turning points in the war. From this time on, Allied forces in the Pacific were advancing toward Japan, not retreating. For a long while, however, it was slow and bloody fighting as Halsey drove northward up the chain of Solomon Islands. Here he and his staff devised a plan of island hopping. If one island was heavily defended by the Japanese, Halsey would simply skip it and strike at another, less fortified island to the north. In this way he could cut off the supplies of the well defended island, leaving the men there "to wither on the vine."

One day in early August, Halsey's operations officer entered his quarters in Nouméa looking worried. "Sir," he said, "three of the torpedo planes that left here to rejoin the *Saratoga* are missing."

Instantly Halsey understood the full meaning of what had happened. Years before his son Bill, Junior had been unable to enter the Naval Academy because of his eyesight; but wartime requirements were not so strict, and with the beginning of the war, Bill had joined the navy. He had been assigned to the

Saratoga, and when the ship was near Nouméa, he had come ashore to visit briefly with his father. Then he had flown off, intending to rejoin his shipmates on the *Saratoga*.

Slowly Halsey asked, "My son — was on one of the missing planes?"

"Yes, sir."

Halsey did not speak, and the operations officer told of the search being made for the missing planes. Still Halsey did not answer, and the officer asked, "Do you have any special orders in this case?"

"My son is the same as every other son in the combat zone," Halsey said. "Look for him just as you would for anybody else." Yet he was aware of a fear deeper and colder than any he had known when the Japanese bombers plunged at the flag bridge of the *Enterprise*.

Day followed day with no word. Then came the message: the men had been found, safe — and the day they were found was a Friday, the 13th! After that, Halsey said, "I spit in the eye of the jinx that had haunted me."

By the late spring of 1944, most of the islands in the South Pacific area had been captured or bypassed. On June 15, Admiral Halsey turned over the command of the area to another admiral and flew back to Pearl Harbor. New duties awaited him.

10. Fleet Commander

When Admiral Halsey returned to Pearl Harbor from the South Pacific, he found things far different than they had been a year and a half before. Back in the United States the tremendous power of American industry had been turned full blast to war production. Ships and planes had poured, as if by magic, from factories and shipyards. Many had gone to join the war in Europe where the invasion of Normandy had just begun. But many had also gone to form a vast and ever growing fleet, striking westward across the Central Pacific. The Gilbert and Marshall Islands had been captured, then Tinian and Saipan.

After the capture of Saipan, Admiral Raymond Spruance, who had been in command of the Central Pacific fleet, was called back to Pearl Harbor to rest and make plans for later action. Admiral Halsey, just back from the South Pacific, was given command of the ships. Under Spruance these had been known as the 5th Fleet. Under Halsey these same ships became the 3rd Fleet. The change in name was to make clear who commanded. It also confused the Japanese who, for a while at least, believed two gigantic fleets were roaming the same waters.

Because he loved carriers, Halsey considered making the old *Enterprise* his flagship. But a carrier is always vulnerable. A single bomb might set off furious fires of aviation gasoline that would wipe out communications with the rest of the fleet. This was a risk the fleet commander could not take. So Halsey moved his flag to the fast, new battleship *New Jersey*.

Plans now called for an invasion of the Palau Islands southwest of Saipan. To confuse the Japanese, Halsey sent one group of ships north to hit the Bonin Islands. With that attack under way, the other ships turned to the Palaus. For three days, from dawn until dark, Halsey paced between the *New Jersey*'s flag bridge and flag plot. He watched from a distance as his planes roared upward from the carriers, banked sharply to the right, took formation, and headed off to bomb and strafe the islands. Through binoculars he watched the planes return, trying to see which were damaged even before dashing into flag plot to get the reports. The planes were meeting heavy antiaircraft fire, he learned, but there had been few Japanese planes and these were quickly destroyed.

With so little opposition, Halsey decided not to keep the main body of his fighting ships at the Palaus to support the invasion. Instead, he left a number of small, escort carriers to furnish air cover. Then on September 8, 1944, the big carriers with their accompanying battleships, cruisers, and destroyers turned still farther west.

They struck Japanese airfields on Mindanao, the southernmost of the Philippine Islands, then swung north, battering other islands. In all these attacks Halsey found the Japanese defenses in the Philippines far weaker than expected. There were fewer planes. Equally important, a great many of the enemy pilots were inexperienced. The long fighting in the Solomon Islands, followed by the battles near Saipan, had simply wiped out the majority of Japan's best pilots.

Halsey knew that President Roosevelt and the chiefs of staff had made plans for General MacArthur to invade Mindanao, then fight his way northward through the Philippines and retake them. But when Halsey considered the weakness of the Japanese defenses, it seemed to him that Mindanao might be by-passed, the invasion staged farther north, and the whole course of the war speeded up.

It was not his business, Halsey thought, to tell Admirals King and Nimitz and President Roosevelt what to do. Still.... He talked it over with his staff, made up his mind, and sent Admiral Nimitz a dispatch.

By luck, Roosevelt and Sir Winston Churchill, the British Prime Minister, were meeting in Canada, and Admiral Nimitz passed Halsey's dispatch on to them. They in turn sent messages to General MacArthur to learn his opinion.

As a result, the invasion of Mindanao was canceled. Leyte, farther north in the Philippines, would be invaded instead.

Under the new plan, Halsey's ships would support MacArthur's troops when the invasion began. But first the fleet would strike at Okinawa and other Japanese bases between Leyte and Japan. In this way they could halt, or at least hinder, the flow of reinforcements from the Japanese homeland.

The schedule called for the fleet to hit Okinawa on October 10, but October is the hurricane, or typhoon, season in the Pacific, and out of the south a giant storm came roaring, also heading for Okinawa. Luckily the center of this storm missed Halsey's fleet

Admiral Halsey supervising the operations of the
Third Fleet from the bridge of the *New Jersey*

and the Admiral was quick to take advantage of it. Even though giant waves marked the typhoon's wake, Halsey assembled his ships as close behind it as possible. The storm made it impossible for Japanese search planes to find the ships. When the weather cleared, Halsey's planes hit Okinawa by complete surprise.

Swiftly the American ships turned south to strike Formosa. Here Admiral Fukudome, the Japanese commander, had 230 fighter planes when the first wave of U.S. fighters roared in the morning of October 12. When the second wave of U.S. planes struck, Admiral Fukudome had 60 fighters left. In the afternoon a third U.S. wave swept over Formosa; not a single Japanese fighter rose to meet them.

Next day the Americans continued to pound Formosa airfields, as Fukudome still had bombers there. In the late afternoon as Halsey was about to head for the Philippines, the Japanese bombers struck back. One plane, hit by AA guns and on fire, crashed into the big carrier *Franklin*, doing only slight damage. Another put a torpedo into the cruiser *Canberra*. She did not sink, but was so badly damaged she had to be taken in tow.

Because the crippled *Canberra* could move at only four knots, there was no chance to get quickly out of range of the Japanese planes. And in the late evening

of the 14th, Admiral Fukudome struck with everything he had.

Out of the gathering darkness, low over the water, the Japanese bombers came by ones, twos, and half dozens. Fighters from the carriers met them far out to sea. Some were shot down, but others kept coming. Standing on the *New Jersey*'s flag bridge, Halsey saw first one, then another, loom black against the sunset sky, met almost instantly by bursting clouds of antiaircraft fire. Planes spun crazily, hit the water,

and burst into flames. As far as Halsey could see over the darkening ocean, red and orange fires blazed horribly. When a ship passed in front of one of these fires it was impossible to tell whether it was the ship or a downed plane that burned.

Actually, only one ship was hit that night. The cruiser *Houston* was torpedoed and, like the *Canberra*, had to be taken in tow. But the Japanese pilots, seeing fires spread all over the dark ocean, radioed that the American fleet had been almost destroyed.

In Japan there was almost hysterical rejoicing. Hour after hour radio announcers told bigger and bigger stories about the U.S. ships that had been sunk. Hitler and Mussolini sent congratulations. And far off in the Central Pacific a lone Japanese plane flew over the Palau Islands, newly captured by the marines. It dropped leaflets that read:

FOR RECKLESS YANKEE DOODLE

Do you know about the naval battle done by the American 58th Fleet on the sea near Taiwan (Formosa) and Philippine? Japanese powerful Air Force has sunk their 19 aeroplane carriers, 4 battleships, 10 several cruisers and destroyers, along with sending 1,261 ship aeroplanes into the sea. From this result we think you can imagine what will happen next around Palau upon you . . .

About this same time Admiral Halsey was sending an equally humorous but more accurate report to Admiral Nimitz in Pearl Harbor:

"All 3rd Fleet ships reported by Radio Tokyo as sunk have now been salvaged and are retiring at high speed toward the enemy."

Ahead lay the greatest naval battle in history.

11. Battle of Leyte Gulf

On October 20, 1944 American soldiers under General MacArthur invaded the Philippine island of Leyte. Halsey, with Task Force 38, was operating just to the north and east in support. At dawn on the 24th he watched as search planes took the air from nearby carriers, then went to his quarters to bathe and shave, being slow about it as usual. Later he was eating breakfast when an officer brought him the message: one of his search planes had located a Japanese force of five battleships, nine cruisers, and about thirteen destroyers to the west of Leyte and headed east.

Halsey pushed back his chair and headed for flag plot. Within minutes his orders had been broadcast.

All ships were informed of the location of the Japanese force. The various task groups were ordered to close formation.

And then the final order, "Strike! Repeat: Strike! Good luck!"

Spread over miles upon miles of ocean, the American carriers turned into the wind and began to launch their planes.

As they took to the air, Halsey received another message: a second Japanese force consisting of two battleships, four cruisers, and a number of destroyers had been located south of the first one.

Bending over their charts Halsey and his staff plotted the Japanese positions. They named the ships to the south the Southern Force, the others the Central Force. Studying their courses, Halsey realized the Southern Force was headed for Surigao Strait south of Leyte. The Central Force was headed toward San Bernardino Strait to the north. If the two forces passed through these straits, they could then swing together on the eastern side of Leyte. And caught between them would be the American ships landing troops and supplies.

It was a good plan, but to Halsey there was one vital part missing. Carriers had proved to be the most powerful ships in the fleet. So where were the Japanese carriers?

"The Japs are not going to attack without them," Halsey said and sent search planes out to look.

By this same time American planes were beginning their attack on the Japanese Central force—and the Japanese ships were without fighters to protect them. Unhurriedly the American planes took position, then roared in: the fighters first, raking the decks with machine-gun fire; then the dive bombers, rolling out of formation one at a time, slashing down like arrows, while torpedo planes drove in from all sides.

Two of the ships in the Central Force were the *Yamato* and *Musashi*, the world's most powerful battleships. Their guns threw up great clouds of multi-colored antiaircraft fire. The American planes bored through it, many of them centering their attention on the *Musashi*. Four torpedoes hit it at almost the same moment. Dive bombers scored hit after hit. Finally, pounded by countless bombs and at least nineteen torpedoes, she turned on her side and went down.

While the air attack on Central Force continued, Halsey sent a dispatch designating certain battleships, cruisers, and destroyers as Task Force 34. This force would be formed only if the Japanese pushed on through San Bernardino. If they did, TF 34 would form a battleline and engage the Japanese in a gun duel while the vulnerable carriers stayed out of range.

Actually TF 34 was not formed. In the late afternoon, while U.S. planes still battered Central Force, Halsey got the news he had been waiting for: four Japanese carriers, three cruisers, destroyers, and two old battleships half converted to carriers, had been sighted. They were approaching from the north, and so they were named the Northern Force.

Faced with three Japanese forces, Halsey now had to decide which to meet head on, and where.

At this time the U.S. had two separate fleets under separate commands operating in the Philippines. The 7th Fleet was small, composed chiefly of old battleships, a few cruisers and destroyers, along with a number of small, slow, escort carriers, all under the command of Admiral Thomas Kinkaid. He would protect the army's transports and supply ships and give close air support to army troops ashore. His commanding officer was General Douglas MacArthur.

The job of Halsey's huge 3rd Fleet was offensive, to strike the enemy wherever he could be found. But during the invasion of the Philippines, Halsey was also supposed to cooperate with the army. His commanding officer, however, was Admiral Nimitz in Pearl Harbor, not General MacArthur.

Even so, the two fleets were in communication and Halsey knew that Kinkaid's battleships were off Surigao Strait.

Leaning over his charts on the *New Jersey*, Halsey figured that Kinkaid's battleships could take care of the small Japanese Southern Force. He believed the Central Force to be so badly damaged it might not actually push on through San Bernardino Strait.

Halsey considered three courses of action:

1. He could guard San Bernardino with his whole fleet and wait for the Northern Force to strike him.

2. He could divide his force, leaving part off San Bernardino to oppose Central Force and sending the others north to meet the Japanese carriers.

3. He could take his entire fleet north and leave San Bernardino unguarded.

Halsey rejected the first plan. He was afraid that if he kept his ships near San Bernardino, planes from the Japanese carriers could attack him while still out of range of his own planes, then fly on to land on Leyte.

He rejected the second plan because, despite the power of his force, he did not want to divide it.

That left the third plan. This was the one Halsey instinctively preferred. He believed with all his heart in attack, striking hard with all he had. And he believed in the overwhelming importance of carriers. He leaned forward and put one blunt finger on the chart. "Here's where we are going." he told his chief of staff. "Start them north."

The 65 fighting ships of Task Force 38 turned north to meet the 17 comparatively small ships of Admiral Jisaburo Ozawa. Behind them San Bernardino Strait lay unguarded.

Unfortunately, there was one part of the Japanese battle plan Halsey did not know. The Japanese carriers approaching from the north were actually a deliberate bait to pull Halsey away from San Bernardino. The Japanese carriers had almost no planes on them because Japan had lost almost all her trained naval fliers. Admiral Ozawa, commanding the Northern Force, expected to lose most of his ships. But if he could lure Halsey away from San Bernardino, the powerful Central Force could slip through and destroy the ships landing men and supplies on Leyte, unprotected, while Kinkaid battled the Southern force. Caught on shore without supplies, the American troops already fighting there could be smashed by Japanese soldiers.

Underestimating the danger to the transports and the baby carriers escorting them, Halsey rushed northward. Now and then dispatches reached him indicating the Central Force was still advancing through San Bernardino. Several of his junior officers suggested that part of the fleet should be sent back to stand guard. Halsey ignored them. All his attention was centered on destroying the Japanese carriers.

Somewhere in the Pacific a bomber receives the signal to take off from a U.S. aircraft carrier.

With dawn the planes of Task Force 38 took the air. At about this same time Halsey received a message from Admiral Kinkaid asking if TF 34 was guarding San Bernardino. TF 34 were the ships that would have formed the battle line had Halsey held his position near Leyte.

Soon there was another message: enemy ships had passed through San Bernardino and were attacking the baby carriers of the 7th Fleet. Where was Task Force 34?

But Halsey was still thinking of his own planes already flying toward the Japanese carriers. And messages soon began to pour in from them. They had sunk one carrier, badly damaged two others plus a cruiser, and the fight was continuing. Now the Japanese ships had turned away and were running north, but the cripples could make little speed. If the battleships and cruisers of Task Force 38 caught them, the entire Japanese force could be destroyed.

At the same time messages poured in from Kinkaid. In desperation the small carriers of the 7th Fleet were calling for help. Where was TF 34?

Then came a message that read:

From: CINCPAC
To: COM THIRD FLEET
THE WHOLE WORLD WANTS TO KNOW WHERE IS TASK FORCE 34.

Halsey stared at it in disbelief. It seemed incredible that his friend Admiral Nimitz in Pearl Harbor would send such a message. To Halsey it seemed like a deliberate insult. He snatched off his hat and slammed it on the deck and his face grew white with anger. He stamped on it, cursing wildly. Admiral Carney grabbed him by the arm. "Bill!" he shouted. "Get control of yourself!"

With great effort Halsey forced his hands to stop trembling. He picked up his cap. Then, his big jaw set, he gave the orders that finally formed TF 34 and sent it, along with several of his carriers, racing back toward San Bernardino. The other carriers kept battering the retreating Northern Force.

Actually it was too late for TF 34 to be of any help to the baby carriers. And it was only later that Halsey learned what had happened.

The battle line of the 7th Fleet had met the Japanese Southern Force as it came through Surigao Strait and totally defeated it, just as Halsey had expected. But the Central Force, not nearly so badly damaged by American planes as Halsey believed, had pushed through San Bernardino and caught the baby carriers by surprise. What followed was one of the most gallant and confused actions of the entire war. Japanese battleships and cruisers hammered the slow carriers and the few destroyers that protected them. Almost every ship in the U.S. force was sunk or damaged. In turn the carriers' planes had struck back at the Japanese ships. Destroyers and tiny destroyer escorts had charged head on at battleships and cruisers, forcing them to slow down and change course while the carriers tried to escape.

Just as the Japanese seemed to have everything won, with nothing between their warships and the defenseless transports, the Central Force had turned and fled. It was only after the war that Americans learned why. The Japanese admiral had been out of communication with the Northern Force. He did not know that TF 38 had been lured away. But he did know his Southern Force had been destroyed. Fearful of being caught in Leyte Gulf alone, he had turned back through San Bernardino.

Altogether the Battle of Leyte Gulf, fought in many separate actions, had been a tremendous American victory. Admiral Halsey would never admit that he had been wrong in taking his entire force north to meet the Japanese carriers, although most naval experts believe he was. Certainly, however, Admiral Nimitz had not intended any insult in his message asking the whereabouts of TF 34. He had not sent the message in the form Halsey received it.

Communications officers usually put a few words of nonsense at the beginning of every message sent in code. This was to make it more difficult for the Japanese to break the code. Nimitz' message had read: "Where is TF 34?" It was the encoding officer who wrote in: "The whole world wants to know."

Years later Admiral Halsey could still get angry thinking about it.

12. Kamikazes and Typhoons

After the Battle for Leyte Gulf, Japan was never able to send any large number of ships to oppose the U S. fleet. In desperation she resorted to a new and terrifying weapon called *kamikazes*.

In Japanese *kamikaze* means "divine wind." Back in 1281, Japan was saved from invasion by a storm — a "divine" wind — that destroyed the enemy fleet. Now the Japanese hoped to create a new type of storm by sending suicide pilots to attack the U.S. fleet. These men planned to fly their planes headlong into the ships, hoping to swap one life and one plane for a U.S. carrier.

Kamikazes struck Task Force 38 for the first time shortly after noon on October 29, 1944. This first attack was small, with only one ship, the carrier *Intrepid*, slightly damaged. The next day, however, they were back in greater numbers. As always, they centered their attention on the vulnerable carriers, but Admiral Halsey, standing on the *New Jersey's* flag bridge, could see them. He watched with a kind of infuriated awe.

The planes came from every direction, some high, some barely skimming the water. These were not the skilled, highly trained pilots who had won so many victories early in the war. Many of them were barely more than amateurs, unfit for combat flying. They made little attempt to fight back at the American planes and most were quickly shot down. But one,

A *kamikaze* blazes on the deck of the *Saratoga* as fire-fighters rush into action.

already afire, crashed close alongside the *Enterprise*. Another dived head on into the *Franklin*. Another hit the *Belleau Wood*. Neither ship was sunk, but both had to limp back to Pearl Harbor for repairs.

On November 25 the Japanese sent out the largest number of *kamikazes* they had used so far. Swarming in from all directions, they broke through the patrolling fighters despite heavy losses. None went for the *New Jersey* where Halsey stood watching, but four carriers were hit. Although none sank, fires and explosions killed men on all four.

By this time the ships and men of TF 38 had been at sea for two months, in almost daily combat. Weariness had become a greater enemy than the Japanese, and accidents due to sheer exhaustion increased. Finally Halsey turned the fleet away from the Philippines and went back to the island of Ulithi for rest and repairs.

There was nothing at Ulithi except a vast, coral-rimmed lagoon, sand beaches, and a few palm trees. But at least the men could sleep without danger of being attacked; they could swim or lie in the sun and rest.

Not so for Halsey. For months he had been getting up at dawn, going to bed at midnight or later. He was sixty-two years old, and most men would have cracked under the constant strain. Halsey had merely grown lean; his big jaw looked longer and harder than ever; his gray eyebrows more bushy. He could still joke—but right now there was very little to joke about. In less than a month *kamikazes* had cost his fleet 328 men killed, approximately 90 planes destroyed, three carriers put out of action, and others damaged.

Something had to be done, and TF 38 had scarcely dropped anchors at Ulithi before Halsey was at work with his task group commanders trying to figure out what.

The plan they came up with had many parts, but the most important was known as the "big blue blanket." The blanket was to be formed by airplanes, and it was to be spread over every Japanese airfield within range of the fleet. The best place to destroy enemy planes, Halsey knew, was on the ground. If he could prevent most *kamikazes* from ever being airborne, then the combat air patrols should be able to shoot down the others.

For two weeks the great fleet swung on its anchors at Ulithi. Then, on December 11, they filed through Mugai Pass—battleships, carriers, cruisers, destroyers, stretching across the blue sea in lines longer than the eye could reach. In his chair on the *New Jersey*'s flag bridge, Halsey sat watching. His uniform was neatly pressed as always, his shoes shining.

General MacArthur's soldiers were fighting on the Philippine island of Mindoro now, and in mid-December Halsey's planes came roaring in to help them. With dawn a blanket of fighters struck at every Japanese airfield within reach—and kept striking. For three full days the U.S. planes attacked. In that time they destroyed an estimated 270 Japanese planes and sank more than 30 ships. Halsey lost only 27 planes. And not a *kamikaze* got within 20 miles of the fleet.

Halsey was beaming happily when, on the evening of December 16, TF 38 turned eastward. His plan was to refuel at sea on the 17th, then swing back to batter the Japanese once more. He had no way of knowing that an altogether different enemy was about to deal his men and ships one of the most vicious blows of the entire war.

A few hundred miles to the southeast of TF 38 a typhoon was brewing. But weather reports were scanty, and the fleet aerologist had no indication of a storm nearby.

Even so, the weather on the 17th was rough. Waves broke clear over the bow of the big tankers. Destroyers were tossed about so that fuel lines snapped. Shortly after noon, Halsey ordered his ships to quit trying to refuel.

All afternoon and night the weather grew worse.

At the height of the typhoon, mountainous waves
swept over the flight deck of the *Hornet.*

Even so, no one realized they were on the edge of a
typhoon. Anxious to return to the Philippines to
support MacArthur's troops, Halsey ordered his ships
to try to refuel again in the morning. Once more the
giant hoses were snapped like threads as the ships
were flung first one way then another.

Refueling was abandoned, and the ships changed
course trying to dodge the storm. Unfortunately for
many of them, the new course took them straight into
the eye of the typhoon.

The *Hornet*'s flight deck finally crumpled under the savage battering of wind and waves.

Winds of more than 100 miles an hour howled about the ships, tore the tops from giant waves, and mixed the sea water with rain in a blinding wall. The waves themselves, sometimes more than 70 feet high, smashed at the ships—first from one side, then another. On some of the carriers the huge flight decks were ripped apart, torn loose, and hurled downwind like leaves in a storm. Later Admiral Halsey would write: "The *New Jersey* once was hit by a five-inch shell without my feeling the impact... yet this

97

typhoon tossed our enormous ship as if she were a canoe. . . . We could not hear our own voices above the uproar."

On the little destroyers the effect of the storm was even more deadly. Some of them rolled until their stacks were parallel with the water, then stayed that way, held down by the wind. Miraculously, most of them recovered. But three destroyers rolled too far, could not recover, and plunged down.

When at last the storm passed, Halsey ordered every ship and every plane it was possible to get into the air, to search for survivors. Amazingly, a few were found clinging to life rafts and floating in jackets. But 790 men were lost. Some 200 planes had been smashed on the carriers' decks, and 28 ships were damaged.

Almost in tears, Halsey radioed General MacArthur that the 3rd Fleet must postpone its return to the Philippines. Instead, the fleet limped back to Ulithi for repairs.

13. TF 38 Hits Japan

Christmas 1944 was spent in the great lagoon at Ulithi, but New Year's Day found TF 38 once more at sea. In the Philippines General MacArthur's troops, moving steadily ahead, were preparing to invade the big island of Luzon, and Halsey gave support by striking air bases throughout the area. Then on January 10, TF 38 sailed through Bashi Channel into the South China Sea.

It was through these waters that most of the oil and vital supplies for the Japanese homeland had to pass. One year before, it would have been practically suicide for an American task force to enter this area, ringed on every side by Japanese navy and air bases. But now, most of Japan's fighting ships lay on the bottom of the ocean. The airfields had few planes and fewer trained pilots. Consequently the sky-blue

planes of TF 38 met little air opposition. Within 10 days they sank or damaged more than 50 merchant ships, wrecked docks, airfields, and supply dumps. On the 20th they swung back toward Okinawa, striking Formosa as they went.

Not an American ship had been damaged in the South China Sea, but as the force passed Formosa, the *kamikazes* came swarming out like hornets. As usual, most were shot down before they reached the ships. But two dived head on into the carrier *Ticonderoga* and another hit the destroyer *Maddox*. Neither ship was sunk, but 144 men were killed.

By the end of January Admiral Halsey had been at sea for 5 months, most of that time in combat. But there was still a twinkle in his blue eyes when, on January 26, he was relieved by Admiral Raymond Spruance.

The twinkle disappeared for a moment when Halsey was handed a dispatch from General MacArthur. It read:

YOUR DEPARTURE FROM THIS THEATER
LEAVES A GAP THAT CAN BE FOULED ONLY
BY YOUR RETURN.

For a few seconds he stared at it, not believing what he read. Then suddenly he burst into laughter.

"I'm not going to get upset over this as I did over Nimitz' dispatch asking about TF 34," he told Mick Carney. "I'll just assume the decoding officer made a mistake." Actually MacArthur's message had read "filled only by your return," not "fouled."

From the Pacific, Halsey flew back to the United States. There he rested briefly and visited his family. He was given a Gold Star in lieu of a third Distinguished Service Medal by President Roosevelt.

By May 7, 1945 when Hitler's army surrendered in Germany, Halsey was back in the Pacific making plans for the invasion of Japan. On May 18 he once more took command of the 3rd Fleet, ready to put these plans in operation.

President Roosevelt's famous smile and a handshake accompanied the admiral's new award.

This time Halsey's flagship was the battleship *Missouri*. As he was piped aboard he was met by Captain Stuart Murray, the *Missouri's* skipper. "This is an important day for me," Halsey told him. "I served on the *Missouri* 40 years ago, and here I am back again."

It was a different *Missouri* now, however, huge and fast. The American invasion of Okinawa had already begun, and the job of TF 38 was not only to intercept the *kamikazes* that flew down from Japan, but to try to stop them before they could ever become airborne. So Halsey took his planes northward to strike at Japan itself. This was what he had yearned to do ever since Pearl Harbor, and he made the most of it. Day after day his planes ranged over the country, battering airfields, factories, railroads. Time after time the battleships and cruisers came in so close to land that Halsey, standing on the *Missouri's* flag bridge could watch the bursting shells.

Only a few Japanese planes rose to meet the blue fighters and bombers of TF 38. Even the antiaircraft was spotty—sometimes extremely heavy, sometimes almost none at all. Weather proved a greater obstacle than the Japanese defenses. Clouds sometimes delayed the attacks. A second typhoon struck the fleet, damaging 33 ships although none was sunk. Once the weather cleared, Halsey attacked again.

On August 6 an Army B29 dropped the world's first atomic bomb on Hiroshima, killing more than 60,000 persons. Three days later a second atomic bomb was dropped on Nagasaki, and shortly afterward Japan began negotiations for surrender. Halsey was informed of this, but not for a moment did he let up his pressure. At dawn on the 15th he launched a strike against Tokyo itself; an hour later a second strike took the air. Halsey watched from the flag bridge until the planes disappeared to the west. Then, as he turned away, he was handed a dispatch:

AIR ATTACK WILL BE SUSPENDED. ACKNOWLEDGE.

Did this mean the war was over? He could not be sure. For the last few days there had been a welter of confusing dispatches. But certainly it meant he should stop his attacks at least temporarily.

"All right," he told his communications officer. "Call the planes back."

He went in to breakfast. It occurred to him that three and a half years before he had been eating breakfast on the *Enterprise* when Doug Moulton, his flag secretary, told him about the attack on Pearl Harbor and the beginning of the war. Since then war had become a way of life. And of death. Hundreds, thousands of young men had been killed following his orders. Others had been burned, blinded, maimed. How many he could not even guess.

Suddenly the door burst open. Doug Moulton, who was now Halsey's Air Operations Officer, burst in. "Admiral!" he shouted. "Here she is!" and threw a dispatch on the table.

It was President Truman's official announcement of peace.

For a moment Halsey could only stare at it. "Victory," he thought. "We've whipped 'em!"

And then: "God be thanked, I'll never have to order another man out to die."

And then he was laughing, shouting, beating all the other officers in the wardroom on the back, and they were beating him on the back, dancing crazily around the room with one another.

It was August 15, 1945, and the war was over.

14. Five Star Admiral

Two weeks after President Truman's first announcement of peace, Admiral Halsey took the ships of Task Force 38 into Tokyo Bay. It was, Halsey said, the "supreme moment" of his career. Dressed as usual in faded but freshly washed and pressed khaki, his shirt open at the throat, he stood on the *Missouri*'s flag bridge and watched the buildings of the city grow clear against the sky. He was grinning broadly when the *Missouri*'s anchor splashed into the bay.

Yet he still did not trust the Japanese. On the ships of TF 38 the men stood at their battle stations. The guns were loaded and ready for instant use. Overhead planes swept back and forth. But the city remained quiet.

The formal signing of the surrender was arranged for September 2 on Halsey's flagship. Early that morning Admiral Chester Nimitz and his staff came on board, then General MacArthur and his staff. Since the Japanese were not due for several minutes, Halsey led MacArthur and Nimitz to his cabin to wait. He knew that in a great moment of history such as this, something impressive should be said. But he could think of nothing. What he said was, "General, will you and Chester have a cup of coffee?"

MacArthur said, "No, thanks, Bill. I'll wait till afterwards."

"So will I, Bill," Nimitz said. "Thanks all the same." And that was it. A few minutes later an officer came to tell them the Japanese were on board.

Even now Bill Halsey could not bring himself to be gracious to a Japanese. He had ordered the sailors on the destroyer bringing the envoys to the *Missouri*, not even to offer them coffee or any courtesy. Admiral Nimitz, who had never felt the deep, personal hatred that Halsey felt, had countermanded the order.

A small table was placed on the deck of the *Missouri* with the formal surrender documents spread on it. Halsey with other Allied officers lined up on one side, the Japanese on the other. MacArthur made a very brief speech, then pointed to a chair at the table and snapped, "The representatives of the

Halsey, center, strides toward the peace table as the signing of the surrender is about to begin.

Imperial Japanese Government and the Imperial Japanese Staff will now come forward and sign!"

The first was the Japanese Foreign Minister. He sat down, took off his gloves and silk hat, dropped his walking cane, picked it up again, looked about as if he could not find a pen. He was obviously stalling, and this made Halsey furious. He felt an impulse to slap the man and shout, "Sign, damn you! Sign!" But he contented himself with merely glaring.

At last the Japanese Minister signed. The other Japanese followed him. General MacArthur, Admiral Nimitz, and other representatives signed for the Allied Powers. Within a few minutes it was done — the long, bloody war was officially ended.

Admiral Halsey had requested that once the war was over he be retired. He was almost sixty-three years old now, and the months at sea, the lack of sleep, the eternal strain, had taken their toll. His hands were shaky. There were deep lines in his face and a pallor beneath the sun- and wind-burned skin.

Halsey was brought back to San Francisco for a tremendous welcome. When he visited his own home town of Elizabeth, N.J., people lined the streets by the thousands to cheer him. Church bells rang and sirens screamed. For Bill Halsey, however, the high point was a visit to the prep school, Pingry School, which he had attended many years before.

Standing on the stage of the gym, Halsey told the boys, "I would give anything I have today to change places with you, to be starting out instead of just finishing up." When the boys stood on their seats shouting, "Halsey! Halsey! Halsey!" he had to struggle to keep from crying.

The Government still had use for him. Halsey was sent on a five week speaking tour of cities in South and Central America. On his return he was promoted

Admiral Halsey waves hello as the mighty Third Fleet steams into San Francisco Bay.

once more—to five star Fleet Admiral, the highest possible rank in the navy and one held by only a handful of men in all history.

Actually, there was little work for him to do. With peace the navy was being dismantled rather than built up. Finally, on April 1, 1947, he was officially retired.

Bill Halsey had led too active a life simply to sit still now and do nothing. He enjoyed hunting, but soon grew restless. He took a job with a large industry, but the work did not seem important to him. Then he found a task he could put his heart into. The government was planning to scrap the carrier *Enterprise*, Halsey's old flagship. Immediately he set out to raise money to save the ship.

This was one fight, however, that Bill Halsey would lose. The old *Enterprise* was turned into scrap iron, although a new, bigger, atomic-powered carrier inherited its proud name. Meanwhile, Bill Halsey had gone to live on Fishers Island, amid the gray waters of Long Island Sound, New York. Here on the night of August 16, 1959 he died quietly in his sleep. He was given a hero's burial in Arlington National Cemetery.

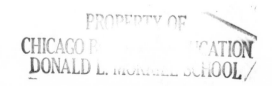

Index